MYSTICALLY GROUNDED

MORDECHAI FLEISING

Published by:

Mordechai Fleising
Ontario, Canada
mordechaifleising@gmail.com

Paperback ISBN: 978-1-927610-01-5
eBook ISBN: 978-1-927610-03-9
Kindle ISBN: 978-1-927610-04-6

Edited by: Baruch Zev Olenick

Cover Design & Layout: Yoel Bender

TABLE OF CONTENTS

PREFACE:

Let me introduce myself to you. My name is Mordechai
Fleising. I grew up in Thornhill, Ontario, Canada,
and am currently living in the land of Israel. In the
mornings and evenings I study the ancient texts with
my study partners and in the afternoons I work as a
Holistic Health and Lifestyle Coach, helping purpose-
driven individuals step up to their life calling through
integrating the different aspects of their life, and giving
them the support to focus in and build grounded
ecology for their personal success.

I grew up with traditional Jewish values, as well as my
share of Canadian/American Western views. I have
been to my share of baseball games, and have had my
times by the local 7-11, drinking slurpees and causing
a ruckus.

My goal in writing this is to stimulate awareness of the greater reality that we are all a part of, both in the global community, and on the individual level, in order for all of us to be able to manifest peace on a global scale.

I begin this work based on a presupposition which follows through the entire content basis of my approach – I, Mordechai, am from a family of priests who descend directly generation after generation, from the High Priest Aharon, the brother of Moshe (Moses), the son of Amram, who descends from Yaakov (Jacob), Yitzchak (Isaac), and Avraham (Abraham), who themselves descend from Shem the son of Noach, who is a tenth-generation descendant of Adam.

Based on this strong chain that has been given over from father to son for thousands of years, through good and bad times, while wandering through the exile since the destruction of the Second Temple, even many times under the punishment of death, do I convey, write, and express my viewpoint. This work is not an academic text, rather one of rich teachings from the heritage and tradition that I have been privileged to be born into.

As a side note, I have decided to transliterate Hebrew names authentically, not using the common transliterations found in English-language literature (e.g. Avraham, not Abraham).

THE CHILDREN OF MAN

Let us begin from the beginning. Adam was created!
The Torah relates more than one version of the creation
of Man, and before we even get started let me preempt
this with a saying of the wise men of the Talmud, that,
"Both these and these are the words of the living God."[1]
While it seems to be that there are two stories, they may
as well be just different viewpoints of the same story.
The initial account is of one man being created as a
whole unit comprising both the male and female sides.
The commentators go into great detail of the excitement

of the universe at his creation. He was so pure that his body shined stronger than the sun[2], his perception of reality was unfathomable, he could see from one end of the world to the other, he was on the conscious level to know the ripple effect reaction of every action in the universe. As it says in the Torah "in the form of God" he was created, to the point that even the angels wanted to worship him[3].

All of the parts of the creation gave of themselves to partake in his creation. From all the lands of the earth was he gathered from, comprising within him the lower levels of the creation which are inanimate, vegetative, and the living creatures, all uniting together in this being that would give their existence conscious meaning. They invested in him to be the vessel of refined physicality together with a Godly spark within him, and the free will to choose truth and reject falsehood, so that the world could be elevated from not just a physical unconscious world, but a choosing and elevating reality. Can you imagine the joy of the universe!

God, or shall we say the "Ain Sof" (Without End, or Infinite one) in His infiniteness, desired (so to speak) to give that which is finite, the ability to, through choice and overcoming of obstacles, progress or move back to what it already was originally, and become infinite by choice. This is the task of man and all of existence is rooting for him.

Well, almost everyone. The snake ultimately gave the world a different angle on how this elevation process will happen. Man needed to fall. In fact, his height was shortened a hundred cubits[4] and he was put into a consciousness more like in the way we perceive reality today, a post-sin-of-Man reality. The job hasn't changed, only the rules of the game. He was kicked out of the Garden of Eden, and instead of being served by angels, he brought death to the world, and was cursed with needing to earn a living through sweat and effort, and his wife was given childbirth pains (the commentators say that before the sin two went into the bed and four came out, pregnancy and birth being instantaneous).

I am not going to place focus at this point on what his sin was, or how he was led into such a grave error, however, I must clearly state that under no circumstances was this matter by chance, and was most definitely an integral part of the Divine Plan. Adam as a whole which included his other half Chava (Eve) was the collective being of every single human in one body. Now, after the sin, death entered the world, and the process of elevating the unconscious Godly sparks in the physical matter of the universe was given as a task for all the children of Man.

Let me fast forward to Avraham. He was born to Terach, who was an idol vendor. From a very young age Avraham saw that the true Divine service couldn't be in worshipping the sun, moon, trees, or other deities that were worshipped as gods at the time. Rather, there must be an original conscious source behind it all. (In previous generations, people began to make the error of thinking that by honoring the sun and stars – the 'servants' of God - they were honoring God. Unfortunately this warped logic led the masses to forget about the Divine service, and to spend their time worshipping the forces of nature and the deities they created for themselves.)

Avraham took it upon himself to fix this mistake and bring the world back to the consciousness that was mostly forgotten since the time of Adam. Avraham and his wife Sarah were world-famous celebrities who attracted a huge following of people to their cause and to the service of the universe. They had a tent that was open on all sides and hungry travelers could always be found there. He, and even more so Sarah, were on the level of prophecy, and were in communication with God. Even though he wasn't commanded to, he was able to learn out actions and Divine laws from his environment, meaning that he was able to intuit on a Divine frequency, and channel himself to the Divine will of rectification, through his prophecy.

Although he and his wife were very successful in their work of spreading the forgotten message of bringing finite to infinity through choice, they were worried that the message alone wouldn't carry through to bring about this global elevation. So God promised them[5] that although it will be difficult, his children will bring about the fixing, and the message will never be forgotten. Those who are not from this lineage but are 'on board' for this Divine mission, are able to connect to the root soul that Avraham claimed, without being an actual blood descendant, in order to be a channel of the Divine will. Nobody is left out of this work. Don't forget that we all stem from the original man Adam, and are, through soul reincarnations, doing a micro-level fixing of some aspect of the original duty of Adam.

THE KABBALISTIC META-SYSTEM

A very important note: As I have heard many times from different Kabbalists, wherever someone begins in the wisdom of Kabbalah, they are always found "smack in the middle". There is no place of beginning. It is the whole nature of the wisdom that it must be digested in a holistic way, and if one thing is taken out of context, it will inevitably be missing a vast amount of information. My goal in these few chapters is to begin "smack in the middle", an attempt to show you the meta-system and how it spans far into every single aspect of our reality, and beyond that.

"From my flesh I can see Divine" is a line in the book of Iyov (Job),[6] which tells us that the way for us to perceive the higher realms and universes that are not physical, are found directly through our ordinary material reality. This means that the system The Infinite One uses to communicate to us, the finite, is through means that function in the same root manner as our own perceptions of reality.

The Kabbalists warn of the great mistake of making those spiritual concepts physical, they are in no way physical! The ability for us to relate to that which is not in our reality is beyond our grasp, so how can we possibly come to know of anything higher than the physical? This is why Iyov tells us that through our very reality we can perceive the system of the universe, as if in the way of a parable.

Now I will explain a great area of discussion between the Kabbalists of many generations, and that is: To what extent is life a parable? Do I exist; is it all just a mirage, or a dream? If everything is one, then why do my actions really make a difference? This also directly leads to the topic of free will, that if God is all then how can I choose? Also, the other side, that if God actually did create a system that is finite, then it is completely finite with no connection to God, and once again, we are faced with a problem that leads people to do whatever they want and claim it to be morally and spiritually acceptable. (We will get into a further discussion of the different manifestations of the sides of this paradigm in a later chapter.)

The answer to these questions is simple; just like the Infinite Light is called "the simple all-encompassing Light". Simply, meaning without a dichotomy or a breakdown into parts, our existence (however complicated it may be) is part of the simple existence. Really, it is a matter of relativity, for a human being who feels and experiences the reality as it seems through the senses, there is no question as to whether or not he may exist. He does. However, the underlying current of our reality is that there is only one God and nothing else, nothing outside of Him. He is all encompassing, and we are found within this infinite system of the universe which has let us call Him "God". (He is also obviously genderless, despite being referred to in the masculine form.) From a higher perspective, there is just God, from my perspective there is just me, and it's my duty to come to terms with this seeming paradox!

MORE ABOUT RELATIVITY

The concept of relativity is very commonly discussed in the texts, especially in the Kabbalistic works. (As we look at the following concepts please keep in mind the Kabbalists' warning against making spiritual concepts physical.) Let's look at an example. There is a man whose name is John Smith. John has a child. John has parents and grandparents. His daughter got married, so he now has a son-in-law and grandchildren. He is married to a lady named Susie. As well, he runs his own business with many employees.

Now let us examine the different ways of relating to this man John: He is a grandson, a son, a brother, an uncle, a cousin, a husband, a father, a father-in-law, a grandfather, and a boss. Let's assume he has a few friends, which makes him a friend. He enjoys painting and therefore is an artist and he volunteers with children in a school and is called a teacher.

This example is a great way of introducing the terms and relationships of terms mentioned in the Kabbalah. If I were to say that John is only a father, would that be true? Or if I would discuss other aspects and leave out his artistic talents, would I be giving a fitting description of John?

John is John. He is a simple entity with many aspects. Depending on the role he is playing, he is referred to by the appropriate name. For his young child he is a grown-up, a big person who probably knows everything there is to know in the world, whereas to his own parents, John is young and has yet a lot to learn.

Does his parents' relationship to John throw out the ideas of the young child? No, the relative reality is that for the child, John really is big and smart, and for the parents, he still is young and has so much to learn. As we can see, both are able to exist in the same moment, from within the same reality, just from different points of view.

In the physical world we see clearly how silly it would be to call John merely a boss. He is way more than that! In the spiritual realms, it is all the more silly to try to isolate one concept and say that something with the label x is only x. This again is where the warnings of making concepts physical are referring, especially in regards of doing this "concept isolation" on a spiritual level.

In truth, it is impossible to conceptualize the essence of God, but we can appropriately term the emanation from God's essence, 'the Infinite Light'. This is already a stage removed from essence since it expresses the light coming from the essence. Even to talk about essence, that too is not the essence. The vastness of the Creator cannot be merely found and looked up in a book that says after such and such a spiritual height, you will reach God's essence himself. That would be quite a finite definition, which is impossible.

Even the term 'infinite' is a relative concept that changes depending on the onlooker, from the angle from which the observation is taking place. One person may look at a problem as completely over their head and impossible, while someone with a bit more experience or knowledge may have the tools to successfully approach and solve such a problem.

For example: Give a young child in the first grade a mathematical problem from a nuclear physics textbook. Will the child be able to solve it? Now, how about a physics major? Presumably, she won't have any problem whatsoever. For her, that problem can be answered with a basic formula that is commonly used as a stepping-stone in order to develop more complex equations.

So, for the child, the simple equation of the college student is in the realm of impossible. Objectively speaking, the problem itself is far from in essence being impossible, it just is what it is, and the label given to it (easy or hard) depends on the perceiver and the relationship in which it is seen. The labels given are only useful for the person outside of the self, how others can relate to that which simply is.

God doesn't have a name. However in order to give us a channel of connection to the Infinite and a path to ascend to infinity, God gave us the use of his names. His names are not Him, as it says in the Patach Eliyahu section of the Zohar.

Infinity, as my Rebbe reminds me, has no relationship. In prayer it is not The Infinite who we call out to. Infinite and finite can have no relationship; the only way for us finite beings to connect to The Infinite is through a chain of relative infiniteness that we can relate to level after level, from our world until infinity.

This system is the names of God that He gave for us to call out to Him with.

In the example of the man John, imagine if one of his employees came in to the office to ask for a raise and instead of calling John "boss", he uses one of his other titles, asking, "My son, can I have a raise?" A bit mismatched? Yes. I highly doubt the man will be getting a raise, unless he is the office clergyman or John's dad.

When we pray we are talking to the same Infinite One. The only thing of practical difference is how we relate to Him. Is he our Father, our King, our Mother, the God of kindness, the God of justice, or the Creator? The names are garments, or actions, through which the Infinite is manifest.

Once again, not to fall into the error of the people before Avraham, and even people today, thinking to serve the names of God, or the manifestations of God. This is idol worship! If a simple man like John cannot be defined through an isolated name, such as "boss", because he is a person underneath all the hats and titles who contains much more than just that, how much more so on a infinite scale does our ability to relate to the Infinite One through names need to be understood as mere manifestations of His one simple existence, which is infinite.

KABBALISTIC NUMBERS

It may appear, for one untrained in the true wisdom of Kabbalah, that the numbers mentioned in the Torah texts are random. One time it will be describing a spiritual level and use the number 1, other times 2, 3, 4, 5, 6, 7, 8, 9, 10, 11, 12, 13, etc. It may seem that the same state or level described may, in different areas of the work, be referred to with a different number. What is going on?

These seeming inconsistencies are an expression of the world of relativity!

Talking about John, when he is wearing a suit, hat, shoes, and glasses, although it doesn't always need to be stated as such, underneath it all, he is a one, simple John. However, when discussing him in relation to his family, the Smiths, we will need to describe him as an aspect or part of a greater unit that contains many details other than John.

What we learn from this is that the ability to analyze and breakdown a subject into the components present (which are necessary for the context currently being observed) depends on the subject of focus in a given moment.

THE WORLDS

Systematically, there is a concept of different spiritual worlds. (As explained previously there are many relative ways to communicate things, so go with me on the track I am taking and the numbers I am using although they are not absolute.) There are five worlds in a system, but here we will mostly work with four. (The one before/ above Atzilut is called Adam Kadmon, and is usually not mentioned because of its fine spiritual nature. In relation to the system of four it is beyond imagination). The first world beneath Adam Kadmon is called Atzilut, which although not easily translated into English, it is the world of nearness to the Infinite Light. In relation to the three lower worlds, this is viewed as a world of completion and perfection. In relation to the lower levels, it is termed Godly, as if it were next to the Infinite. There is no evil found in this state.

The next lower world is the world of Beriyah, the world of Creation of something from nothing. This world is where evil begins, where the opportunity of 'otherness' starts its manifestation. The darkness and evil is only a small part of this world; mostly the world is Godly and pure with a bit of evil.

The next world is the world of Yetzirah, the world of Formation. This reality is comprised of both light and Godliness, with evil that hides the light. It's a half-light, half-darkness view!

The last of the four worlds is the world of Asiyah, the world of action. This world is mostly dark, with a bit of light. We are found at the end, or bottom, of this world!

THE LEVELS OF SOUL

The soul of all things can also be broken up into five, just like the complete system of worlds can, ranging from the most pure and Godly to the most physical. The following chart gives the names and their corresponding sefira and world.

Level	Corresponding world	Corresponding Sefira	Corresponding letter of the Hebrew alphabet
Yechida	Adam Kadmon	Kesser, meaning the crown which is not part of the system but on top	The top of the letter Yud, only hinted to in the first letter in the Tetragramatton
Chaya	Atzilut World of nearness to the Infinite Light	Chochmah, wisdom, masculine	The letter yud itself, the first letter of the Tetragramatton
Neshama	Beriyah, creation	Bina, knowledge, feminine	The letter Heh, the second of the Tetragramatton
Ruach	Yetzirah, formation	Tiferet, beauty, masculine	The letter Vav, the third in the Tetragramatton
Nefesh	Asiyah, the world of action	Malchut, manifesting kingship, feminine	The final Heh, the final letter in the Tetragrammaton

THE SEFIROT

There are ten sefirot, which are the vessels that are used by the Infinite to relate to us, the finite (as explained previously, regarding the names of God). The number ten is the highest single number that shows a perfect set without being doubled. Twenty would just be two × ten. The Book of Formation says that the number of sefirot is specifically ten not nine, ten not eleven[7].

A perfect whole made out of separate parts. Ten!

DETOUR TO THE NUMBER 3

Everything in matter has three parts: a head, middle, and an end, or, in other words, a top, a middle, and a bottom. There is no such thing as only a top and a bottom. They inherently need to be connected by a middle. So too, there is no bottom and middle without a top. This is the introduction to the famous Kabbalistic number three!

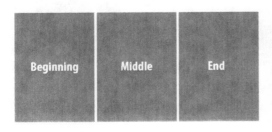
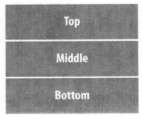

A three dimensional object has the three parts (head, middle, tail) for its length, three for its width, and three for its depth. That brings us to nine individual aspects of one simple object.

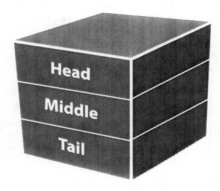

If we go further and focus only on one aspect, let's say the head, we can break it down into another set of three.

So we see that everything can be broken down into sets of threes until infinity. But then how do we get to ten?

When we are looking at John, who is wearing a suit, socks, glasses, shirt, tie, we don't see an assortment of parts. We just see John. When something is viewed in and of itself as a whole unit, it is not just a sum of its parts, which would be 3×3, or nine. Rather, the entirety of it is greater than its sum. This "greater" is the tenth.

For example, a car is made up of an engine, steering wheel, brakes, seats, windows, gasoline, etc. Any of those things mentioned are all in their own right complex items and may be very expensive, but their true function and purpose will only be manifest as they function well together as a one entity called a "car", that drives.

Let's say that the car is no longer functional, yet the brakes still work. Do we view the brakes as part of the broken car? Or how about we take out whatever is useful and assess the value of each element as a single piece that was part of a greater whole, the driving car! Even more so if absolutely nothing works, and all that is left are the screws that are in all the different parts of the broken car! To summarize: Not only does the car as a whole not work, but even the specific units which make up the car are shot, so we look even further into the parts and find the screws, which are useful.

Are you beginning to see the threes? Nine is only 3×3, but ten is the smallest way of including fragmentation, yet still remaining a single unit. The number one is a stand-alone, complete and whole without the parts. One hundred is merely ten × ten. Are you with me now?

So in regards to an infinite being (who encompasses all) to be able to communicate and establish a relationship with the finite, what better number than ten! And there you have the ten sefirot. Like the names of God, they are as well just a bridge for us to be able to relate to Him through. They are Godly, but are not God. To worship one of the sefirot is to commit the sin of idol worship, and frankly it's just missing out on the bigger picture, wouldn't you say?

A bit more about the numbers before we get into the specifics: We systemize the sefirot just like in the charts of threes before, where there is what we call a right column, left column, and central column. There are no graphs and charts in the spiritual realms so all of this stuff is just ways for us to talk about and categorize spiritual functions through the lens of our reality. The left column of sefirot (even though looking at it as part of this system of three), if analyzed on its own, can now become a face in and of itself with a right, left, and center. With a different outlook of the breakdown of the specific names and characteristics of the previous group that contained three, they can now be looked at as ten and include all the characteristics of all of them. So, what was the 'left' is now a right, a left, and center, in and of itself.

FROM MY FLESH I WILL SEE THE DIVINE

Now that we did some meta-math Kabbalah, let's see what the human body has to tell us about the sefirot and the spiritual worlds. Everything in our reality is made up of a two-sided relationship of male and female. Giver-receiver, day-night, hot-cold, these are all pairs of distinctive opposites. They form a system between themselves in which they both need each other for the other's identity. If the giver doesn't have with whom to share, then he isn't much of a giver. In fact, in the pursuit of his needing to give, he becomes the receiver; the needed becomes the needy.

In my own body, according to the Kabbalah, the right side is the male, and the left is the female. Certain commandments are specifically to be done with the right hand, which is the hand of kindness, the giver. The left hand, on the female side, is the hand of restraint, the receiver. Does that mean that an actual woman is viewed as completely receiving? Is she, so to speak, a lefty?

No of course not! Although she has a dominating element of the female side, within her are both elements, just like a man. I mean almost like a man!

In the meta-system of threes described earlier, if the

right is the masculine, and the left is the feminine, what could the central column be? This is the column of knowing, integration, and synthesis between the two.

As we have stated; if there is a top and bottom then there must be a middle. This is the trading point where the two opposites exchange sides of similarity through which they are able to be united as a whole unit. Let's say it is the meeting place of the more manly traits of a female with the womanly traits of a male. There always needs to be a point of connection between two things in any relationship. This doesn't take away from each other's identity, but rather gives them an even stronger sense of self in combination, through this trading off of traits.

Let's give another example, let's say of a father who is a great artist and sculptor. While his son's drawings mean more to the father than anything else in the world, with regards to style, it may be that the father would rarely, if ever, draw on such a basic level. And the son sees his father's grand sculptures, but really loves it when the father draws him a simple picture of a big-wheeled school bus with some crayons.

We just described a place of meeting in the world of art between the two involved in this particular relationship. That which is considered a bad day's work in the father's eyes (in relation to his level) is prized and loved by the child. And that which is the best and most amazing from the child is the lowest that the father would find himself creating. This is the common ground on which relationship between the two can possibly exist in this particular scenario!

This is as well a male-female relationship even if both parties are male. Let's say that a friend of mine is into heavy metal music, and I have other interests. If I am planning on starting a conversation with him, it may be wise to begin regarding those things that I know about from his world, even if to me they are absurd. That bit of conversation will be very meaningful to him, and from there we can further build our relationship, with more pieces of things with which to relate to.

Regardless of topic, different people come across in different ways. It could be about politics, or high prices, with one person sharing his opinion that comes much more from the right hand perspective, while the other is viewing things from a left hand perspective. That is fine and natural, we don't all need to have the same views on every discussion, and people are entitled to their own unique view of situations.

Believe it or not, the two sides of the discussion (let's say of politics) require the other's opposition in order for their own position to be valid. It takes two to tango, as they say. And the things that give them the ability to argue, however ugly the discussion may turn out, are those things that are already agreed upon by both sides as truths. They can argue about everything else under the sun, but if an exchange between the opposing sides isn't happening, no discussion can even begin.

The same is all the more so true for building positive relationships. It is important to just stop and realize the fights we may be finding ourselves in and how our side of the story is a completion of the other side, and if they wouldn't be as strongly opposed to my ideas then I wouldn't have as much power to be doing what I am doing. Even if the opposing party is a hundred percent right, if my pursuit of truth is not out to destroy that other side and I am truly looking to move forward in general for the sake of both parties, then with precise wisdom it is possible to disarm these situations. (Paul Watzlawick calls this 'second order change' in his book Change).

In school I remember hearing the idea that every action has an equal and opposite reaction. A system is a unit and when the right side grows, so does the left. This applies on a small scale of a person with their own life and inner struggles as well as on global crises. The nuclear arms race is a great example that when one side increases, the other does the same and even more, which causes more opposition, etc.

This is not just a science, or a spiritual tradition, this is the God-given key and the formula to manifesting peace in the world. I don't see it any other way!

Unfortunate to mention, but I need anti-Semitism for me to be a real Jew. If I was strong in my identity and didn't have any deep self-doubts about what I am working to accomplish in the world, who is to say that the Jew-haters out there would have something on me to start?

We relate on a certain element (in my mind it is a tiny dot on the edge of my consciousness) saying, "Why should I bother? Why so many commandments? What have I done wrong to deserve all this junk?" Then along comes some idealist terrorists who completely agree with that one thought I am having, and in the relationship between the two, there is what to begin the tension.

There is an expression that every lie has a bit of truth. Why do you think that is? There must be some ground of connection, no matter how minute, in order to begin exchange or argument. Just see for yourself how this concept is manifest in every single relationship of elements in the world, even in chemistry, how the exchange of particles takes place.

The Kabbalah is using these concepts repetitively to bring us to the consciousness of the system of our reality, through which with proper use we can establish peace in our lives and in the world. So many are not in the slightest aware of how things relate to one another. While yes it is a foundational concept in the Kabbalah, it is seen clearly in the world, without needing any revelation from Elijah the prophet to give over these concepts[8].

Consciousness! Make it more than just knowledge, take it as a message for yourself, seeing how all of reality flows according to these set principles, and allow the point to settle in to your heart, not just the mind, of how this can be applied in worlds way beyond the perception of our physical world, and how the same truth is manifest in albeit different ways, in the same form.

Iyov said it, "From my flesh I can perceive the Divine". This is the formula in the form of knowledge. Hopefully with constant practice, I will at least make it my goal to bring it into my heart, into action, this formula.

Knowledge of chemistry is great and an important endeavor, making great findings in medicine and other such areas. But why not let these ideas spread away from the chemical lab into our interpersonal lives, into the political arena, business dealings?

Boy oh boy have we forgotten. Does this sound mystical to you? It bothers me to hear that from people, "mystical"! How about "practical"! I can now really see reality in the way it really is, and I am sure no one will argue with this. The question is only how far to take it, and why not take it all the way to the heavens, and higher?!

It is all about relationships, everything - internal, external, all communications and interactions of the two sides, which are as well only part of a single simple entity. Why not mindfully become aware of it! Not so called "personal work", or pumping people up with encouragement (which is although necessary at times), but awareness of the tools needed to build good relationships, through the understanding of that which is! Period!

Universal truths will stand strong unshakably, while we may be searching in every nook and cranny for answers in the area of mystics, and so-called "spirituality". The answer does lie in the number three, and what its significance is in relation to me. Peace is the reconciliation of opposites, finding the balance point from where to begin the work in a given situation.

Awaken slowly, as you are already on the path of integrating these ideas into your own life, one layer at a time, getting more and more adept at seeing the two sides clearly and on what they are relating. It has already come naturally to you in many expressions in your life, and now as you are reading this it is already becoming a larger area of exploration as to the approach that may have been used in less-than-successful circumstances, for yourself, or others around you, and how it may be circumvented in future situations.

COMMUNICATION

I remember when I was studying in post-high school Talmudic learning, I was reading a commentary on the Zohar, and very excitedly began a discussion with a friend regarding a certain particular detail of how God interacts with the world. Just then, it became so clear to me, as if I was high on the strongest drug, that God is a teacher, God is trying to communicate to us, there is an amazing system set up for this communication, He is not forcing it upon us, it is in our hands.

God wants us to be Godly, which is done by following in the ways of God! What are His ways? The Kabbalah is all about the ways of God, how God "dresses up" Himself, for us to relate to Him. How can I dress my actions up in a more Godly way? Not dress up in a sense of being exterior and not penetrating into the deepest part of my essence, but dressing up so as to communicate an effective message to the audience I wish to approach, be it to a million people, or just my own inner chaos and conflicts.

Communication coming from a stronger place then just the one side of the story which I am talking through, a truly holistic communication, giving the other party a place to be, his right to exist, hearing both sides because they are truly inseparable. It isn't all about me, even though that is my feeling in the matter. There does happen to be a greater picture, and my success depends

on seeing that, and even empowering the opposition
to see his own true picture, not letting selfish emotions
cloud the process of peace.

FOR ME THE WORLD WAS CREATED

Every being needs to have this thought etched into
their psyche. People these days are unfortunately found
without any faith whatsoever, and who can blame
them with all the troubles and wars that have been
fought in the names of faith. Many suffer with deep
inner questions of their worth, and meaning, existential
insecurities. Where am I heading? What is my purpose?
Does there need to be one? Maybe everything is just
blah and is supposed to stay that way?

I read an amazing book by a doctor Victor Frankl called
Man's Search for Meaning. He went through living hell
in the death camps at the hands of the Nazi Germans,
and was able to come out with a positive message
for humanity and learnings and teachings that are
products of his suffering.

He says that a person needs to have a vision in the
small and big areas of life, something that creates
meaning that makes the suffering worthwhile.
Something to have that they would give their own life
for; this is what keeps man alive. Such strong vision. He

mentions that sometimes people are depressed only because they have no vision. He even mentions how the image of his beautiful wife kept him going in the death camps even though he knew she was no longer amongst the living. Just an image can give someone a reason to exist, to fight more than even thought physically possible, in order to live with the vision. Viktor Frankl quotes the words of Nietzche saying that "he who has a why to live for, can bear with almost any how."

The media these days portrays all sorts of realities, fictional or factual, depicting scenes of intense passion, be it religious, political, or even of romance. Bombarding us with these tales of many peoples, parties, or lovers - these "why's" that we have just spoken of.

After a good film I cannot help myself from feeling that strong satisfaction of this external raison de etre, purpose for existence.

Why should Peter Pan's pursuit of "Never Never Land" leave me feeling powerful doing what I do in my life? Am I living a life so shallow, that the film is more real than the struggles and successes of my existence? In tough times, that which will propel me forward will not be coming from a Hollywood production, it will need to stem from a part of my being that is more real to me than anything else in the world. I apologize for dwelling on the subject but just to observe the tremendous power of the movie and media industry, bringing people to tears, to laughter, to fear, and giving over life messages over an hour and a half.

Powerful!

Each person has a unique story that is just as full of humor, fear, overcoming of obstacles, and hopefully will last for a hundred and twenty years.

The Sages of our tradition teach that a person must tell himself that the whole world was created for me![9] To say, that what I have to offer in my existence makes a difference. The value of life! Many may look at life as a means to an end, being some promised prize or heavenly bliss for which they work and suffer all their days towards in blatant misery. On the opposing extreme, there are those who may say "Live and be merry because tomorrow we will die."

Stop!

Break out from the either/or of these paradigms, and see the intrinsic value of the very moments of your life, every defining instant that only uniquely you are given the opportunity to experience, even the utmost simple of tasks, doing the dishes maybe. Or how about just sitting waiting for the bus when it is late in arriving?

Either of those two approaches just don't hold water for being your most and best. I know and am telling you, standing on the shoulders of these great and holy Sages, that every individual deserves that the world be created solely for them, that their exclusive purpose is worth the world, there is meaning in it all. The pains that may be suffered throughout the course of one's lifetime are not just a happenstance, unfortunate occurrence; rather they are of utmost meaning in the drama that is life. Nothing is empty and without meaning!

I mean really why not, walking down the road, or doing the laundry, can't I be in a state of bliss from the realization of my inherent importance, and not in just the major things I may do, but even in the more mundane? My expression is highly valued. Straight healthy thinking as it seems to me anyways.

Rule to remember: If I exist it means I am needed.

Even if one is found in the pits of hell, behind bars, or who knows what it may be, as long as there remains a single breath in his body there is vast significance to his existence. Don't ever forget that. You think God hasn't figured out how to use those lightning bolts as portrayed in the cartoons? Or maybe it is just that until my time is good and ready to leave this world, I still have quite an integral job to do!

Mere existence itself is astounding, as King David says

in Tehilim (Psalms), "The dead can't praise God, nor can those who descend to the gates of hell."[10] It's not about whether I can or cannot be doing the action of praising of God, that's not what I think it is referring to. What it tells me is that as long as you are alive there is hope. And not a hope in a salvation of some sorts, but simply put, hope, and belief that a task is at hand, **and without you it will never be corrected, that's why you are here!**

Let us talk more about our universal responsibilities now that we all know how necessary we are. Rabbi Nachman of Breslov says on this passage of the Sages, that each person must take it upon themselves to pray for the wellbeing of the world. It was created for you, you are the king, and must, to your best ability, take care of that with which you have been entrusted.

The Book of Trembling (written several hundred years ago in the city of Safed) from the Kabbalist Rabbi Elazar Azkari talks about the matter, that if a catastrophe occurs in some distant part of the world, then I need to ask myself, "What have I done to cause this to the world?!"

We as well find with Rabbi Yehoshua Ben Levy, that Elijah the prophet would frequent him at night from heaven to teach him wisdom, and as result of a man being killed by a lion several miles away, Elijah didn't come to visit the Rabbi, since he should have been praying that no accidents should occur in his surroundings[11]. This is a portrayal of a high level of sensitivity that was demanded of Rabbi Yehoshua. Elijah expected a man of his stature to be more in tune with his surroundings, and looked upon this incident as directly being a result of his lack of concern.

These are high ideals but the message rings clear to all. The importance of who I am, should in no way, heaven forbid, be of cause to my lack of concern for others and the global environment. Inversely, my own self worth is what gives me this grand liability to concern myself with the wellbeing of my universe and all its inhabitants.

OK, SO NOW WHY ME?

At the beginning, we discussed our origins and the creation of Man, gathered up from all the elements of the planet, all comprising him, and joining in with him, to partake in global salvation, in the mission of bringing that which is an unconscious manifestation of God's infinity back to its original state of being conscious and infinite through choice. This means elevating the physical world of inanimate, vegetative, and animal kingdoms through the free will of man, to consciously choose good, to avoid evil, and to build a dwelling place for God in even the lowest place.

Now, how can this grand mission be accomplished?

Through man! By investing into man a Godly soul, as it says, "And he breathed into his nostrils a soul of life." He didn't give this job to the heavenly angels, but to us humans who are prone to error, and have had our fair share of blunders through the ages. As I have heard from one of my teachers, animals don't have struggles with their identity. A dog won't look in the mirror and think he is a cat. But humans are constantly struggling with who they are!

We have a part of us which is like the rest of the world, like any other animal, and then to really confuse things there is a spark in us that is a piece of God! So we need to work with what we have to be able to truly express ourselves as who we truly are, not what we label ourselves as, and to step up to refining ourselves in a more Godly manner with the tools we have at the time, and in doing so to elevate all of the unconscious and disintegrated elements in the universe back to their original true identity of being infinite, all through the choice of man!

At the end of the day, living is about the freedom we do have to choose, and our lack of motivation is quite literally part of the game.

DEALING WITH THE MADNESS -
TOHU & TIKKUN. CHAOS & FIXING.

As examined and explained previously, in every
relationship there are always two opposite forces with
a third one in the middle which bridges them. This is
applied to many different sets of systems and patterns
in Kabbalah. The pattern we will look at now is the
spherical-upright (straight) duality. It also contains the
aspects of male-female, active-passive, etc.

It is spoken of in regards to the five worlds discussed
earlier, as well in regards to the ten sefirot. The ten
sefirot actually manifest in both the spherical and the
upright. It is explained in the beginning of the texts
that whenever there is mention of the worlds, or of
the sefirot, it is generally talking about the upright. So,
any Kabbalist, when learning the Zohar, will know to
apply this unmentioned piece of information in most
of the situations.

If you look around, you will notice that squares are
generally not found in nature. All natural objects are
mostly arrayed in circular fashion - trees, flowers,
plants, and animals, all without such commonly
found sharp ninety-degree angles. Nature in its
beautiful, flowing artistic expression, streaming
seamlessly from one scene into the next, the words
"natural" or "organic" call to mind a raw image of

something unaltered by anything foreign to its regular environment, a fruit tree, its fruit scattered around the base of its trunk. It just is, and that is beautiful, the nature of things how they are, entire planets in motion dancing through space.

The world of natural order is spherical. So where does the upright and straight come in? What is its place in our physical setting and in the spiritual worlds? And why is the mention in the texts focused mainly on the straight, while the spherical is barely referred to?

This picture which I have attempted to provide for you is a scenario in which a rectification is meant to occur, the uplifting of the worlds, its refinement through the actions of man, lifting the entire universe back to its original dance of shining Godliness, making manifest God's presence in all things, creating a dwelling place for Him amongst the finite. This is man's mission, in fact, to prepare a dwelling place in the darkest spiritual real estate around!

The lowest sefira is called "the Divine presence in exile" a.k.a. the Shechina. It is a garment of the Infinite with the characteristics (metaphorically speaking) of a woman crying over her lowly situation, and yearning to once again be reunited with the higher sefirot, her husband (a more refined state, comparatively speaking, to that of the garment called the Shechina).

Her persona is the most spoken of from all the spiritual characters, and of course these terms given are just ways for us humans to be able to relate and appreciate, on a more humanistic level, so to speak, the emotions of a mother crying out for her children!

Whenever any holy act is done a small short preparatory prayer is uttered (some just say it once at the beginning of the day), stating that through this act which I am now about to do I am having in mind to pick the Shechina up from the dust, and connect her with the higher sefirot. This is the task of those ready to stand in service of the Creator under the wings of Avraham, to do their work by doing a fixing of the Divine presence in exile, truly an aspect of God in exile, portrayed as this crying, longing woman.

The Shechina is also represented in the final letter in the ineffable name of God.

THE INFLUENCE UPON NATURE

This is something I want to discuss more at length in a later chapter, but briefly there are some who are aligned with the world view of the Kabbalistic systems as have been basically described so far in this work, but would rather leave out the element at hand, being "the straight" (of the spherical-upright duality), which is mainly the aspect discussed in our tradition.

Nature is so full of beauty and ease, everything in
harmony, even the harmony of chaos, the order of the
jungle is so perfect and graceful. Everything knows
its place in the chain. The gazelle is prey to the lion,
while no one looks upon the lion as a murderous
creature, for it simply is doing that which it naturally
does, instinctively! This is an aspect of spherical
reality. However, when told to a human being that
his existence has more than just a natural spherical
component, it can be morally challenging to accept, and
in turn to begin living in a way of specific boundaries
and guidelines.

Spirituality doesn't mean anything to me in that regard;
it is missing half of the picture! Quite an important
half, as the Divine presence (Shechina) wanders lonely
through the streets of the world crying and yearning,
and many are flocking to things of a spiritual nature,
for which the journey this spiritual message was meant
to accompany is forgotten.

I have read that in past times the Talmud was always
under attack, and many times burned publicly,
the opponents claiming that the misdirected and
uninformed Talmudic scholars were lost to the spiritual
nature of things and were left holding the empty shells,
whereas they the oppressors had the soul of what our
tradition is expressing through the Talmud, and so they

felt the need to find and burn as many as they could get their hands on.

Isn't it obvious? The fact that my soul is holy is no novelty, it is true! And the soul will never die! But my poor body, which can only hope to last at most until a hundred and twenty years, can it even be perceived that holiness is a possibility for it? In one place, the Zohar says very simply that the soul loves the body![12] The part of us that is Godly and is never touched by sin, sees in the animalistic side of man pure potential that the soul can never manifest in any way without the help of the human body, in the service of the universe!

To make a blessing before eating a fruit picked fresh from a tree, or giving charity from hard-earned money. The soul delights in this opportunity of growth, an infinite potential!

How much agony must the soul go through for those who are drawn to the spiritual but abandon the physical applications of what is being taught? This is a very common scenario, and in fact very much linked to the reason of the secret nature of this wisdom. Kabbalah was kept under very tight guard only being taught to the extremely righteous only after having learned previously all the areas of the revealed wisdom of the Torah. Yes it is true these concepts are not for everyone to digest so easily, some need things to be laid out much more simply, and all the truth at once may drive them crazy, or bring them to far extremes due to errors in this study.

Kabbalah inherently includes a discussion of the map of how religions and philosophies fit into the grander system, everything neatly settled in its rightful place. And all views do have their rightful place, even the very view of ignoring the influence from outside of the natural spherical order, which helps to define that which is upright and true. A piece of the puzzle which in perspective can be looked upon as a great explanatory view of certain elements, is not necessary the proper foundation upon which to build movements on these parts of a grander scheme!

Rabbi Nachman of Breslov, who has a book full of tremendous novelty in the realm of Kabbalistic thought, says, "Do whatever you want with my ideas but don't change one detail in the Shulchan Aruch (The Code of Jewish Law)!"[13] The changing of a detail in that highly sensitive realm would be the defeat of the entire purpose of our mission here as a people, which is, through action and choice, to lift the Divine presence up from the dust. We are fixers on both the microcosmic and macrocosmic levels. The world is not ours to use and exploit, we should be tending to and enhancing it through our global endeavors.

We have in us both of these aspects as well; the body is spherical, while the soul blows its upright message through our bones telling us that there is more than just this! Don't settle for less, it is settling for infinitely less!

In regards to sin, when a person falls into an immoral act, he is further putting his own aspect of the soul, correlating to the Divine presence, more into exile. And through his true repentance he brings the aspect of Divine presence in himself out of the dust, and into the arms of her beloved.

God gave us specific instruction on how to go about our existence, as was told to Adam, placed in the garden "to work it and to guard it,"[14] corresponding to things that are commanded to be done, and things that are warned to stay away from. On every level there is comprised (relatively) within it both an active and passive state. The role of the active is to give over and build the passive. So whereas in one world it is considered the giver, from the perspective of a higher realm it is a receiver. What this means is there is always what to fix and what to work with. Everything beneath the Infinite is relatively in need of fixing; there is always room for improvement!

Let's say that a person sets his goal this year to earn a certain income. When he reaches his goal, he begins to feel his needs expanding to a different goal, and unless he gets there he won't be happy. When the Sages say that a person will die and never get to even half of his desires fulfilled,[15] this is referring to physical desires, and all the more so in the realms of wisdom!

That level, which was once viewed as a height, is today's average or even low. The present state in any case is what is in a spherical regard, and what it is to be fixed to become in the future is done through the active element of the "straight and upright" component.

An outside influence acting on a system to advance it to a newer peak!

Who can even, let's say, imagine what life was like a hundred years ago, imagine the contrast of scenarios, think about this while fixing a broken iPhone, or being stuck in queue on the runway in a plane. The problems for which solutions are necessary now, would be an unfathomable solution to the problems being faced then! Similarly a vaccine that was used for the previous bug may be obsolete for the new acclimated flu of the next season.

There is no situation one can possibly find that doesn't have a possible improvement and rectification. This is definitely a test of will, and obviously cannot be intentionally done, as it says in the Talmud, "Someone who says God forgives, is forgiven from the world!"[16] This means that a person who uses God's forgiveness as an excuse to do whatever evil he wants, it is as if he loses his right to exist.

The point is to be doing correction of the 'what is' on whatever level you are presently found. And if you fall, there is no place to ever give up hope. Only that situation that was not available previously to a Godly revelation in your life through whatever challenge that had arisen, placed you in perfect opportunity to correct and bring back to the light of unity.

Although it is a great place of opportunity to lift up heavenly sparks in areas devoid of light, the wise men warned and prohibited someone to say "I will sin, and then I will return to the light, thereby freeing fallen sparks hidden amongst the appearing darkness of evil!" They say it is prohibited because, he is not naturally given the ware withal to return, and ultimately his ability to repent will be out of his hands, since repentance is of a higher nature. A preemptive guideline for those searchers of the holy sparks: Always make sure you have a safety net with you in every situation of impending test!

REINCARNATIONS

If a person is not able to accomplish the job in that lifetime, they need to return and finish it up. This may sound very dark and spooky along with images of the barbecue pits of hell with people yelling and being chased by pitchforks. Who knows? But taken out of context of the greater picture, hell and reincarnation sure are a bummer. How does it sound if expressed instead in terms of the finding of oneself?

A man took the seventy-year stroll through life and at the end came out with a large savings account from his lifelong hard work. In his youth, he was a promising student in the university and was well honored. The people wondered where his many talents would take him and what achievements would flower forth. Then he started a small business and made it quite big, and quickly with his keen intellect learned ways of using manipulation to achieve a higher level of success in business.

And so was this man's life, until he died of a heart attack on the golf course. Of what good use did he put his inherent talent and skills? Did he uncover his true self that so many others in his young years remember him as being, up and coming in the world?

How will the soul of this man respond to a view of that which he could have achieved in his time on earth, the potential he had to uncover the masks that he wore from different events in his childhood, or some beliefs he was given, to a place of inner truth and overcoming of limits from the self and the outside world? The loss of the kingdom he was able to build in those very years that he squandered as a workaholic, and a deceiver, how painful that image must be, how much he has fallen short!

Yet in our lives, we all (even the greatest) are going to see this image of our infinite selves that we came to reveal and have still but have fallen short. That is a picture of hell if not worse!

However, don't give up, not even on this man spoken of. There is actually a verse in the Torah that says, "nothing is eternally pushed away[17]", which the Kabbalist Rabbi Moshe Chaim Luzzato in The Tree[18] discusses as referring to the rectification of everything in the universe. Even the most ghastly will be able to return, no matter how long a process of return it takes, to face the light once again.

There is a chapter in the Talmud regarding those who have no share in the World to Come and are completely cast away.[19] Taken literally that's what it says! However, the commentators bring that even those have their correction.

So the choice is in my hands: Do I express that which I have to share and accomplish, or fight against it? Do I challenge my real true self, by choosing evil to the point where not only is reincarnation necessary to return to self, and that even hell may have no correction in the situation? But however it may come about, the system will integrate and recycle all, in the cosmic process of actualizing infinite potential. You choose how it will come about!

REINCARNATED, YOU TOO?

All those, by choice or not, involved in the fixing of the worlds, stem from the original man Adam. He was the inclusive being with all the souls united in him as one. We individuals now represent a single spark and aspect of his entirety. As we discussed above, any object in matter that has a beginning, middle, and end, can further be dissected ad infinitum! The souls from the original soul of Adam are the same. There are souls that are higher root souls and have many sub-souls from their soul group stemming from them, and so on.

The purpose is correction, and by everyone doing their specific part, the process of fixing is underway, bringing the world, collectively this time, to a pre-sin of Adam state, and the sky is the limit where things will sail from there, realities that we cannot even fathom, in pursuit of even further higher refinement, from potential to actual through the finite en route to infinite.

The journey is infinite! But let us not focus on things that we cannot possibly build vision towards. Let's better dwell on the goal at hand that is unfortunately mostly forgotten in today's world, as it has been time and time again, with every renewal, this time hoping to gather together for a global endeavor. The time has come wouldn't you say?

The Sages say that for whoever the Holy Temple is not built in his days, it is as if it has been destroyed in his days.[20] Meaning, with the power that we as individuals have collectively to get our acts together to make a place for the Divine in our lifetimes, surely we will achieve it. If we are not in pursuit of things that drive the redemption of mankind further away from us, then we are intrinsically moving towards it.

Awaken the masses! Realize we are not all just distant cousins, but are all pieces of the same soul harmoniously marching to the same heartbeat!

The opposition needs to learn its place this time around, to realize that there are different sides of the coin, just different sides of one body. Maybe all the wars fought were in response to the lack of communication of the different roots of the different sides of one body? Let's say the male and female sides of Adam the collective soul. Do I attack my arm with my left side, out of anger for that which the right has done?

Have you ever noticed that on days where you feel like you are at the top of the world, everyone around you appears to be that way as well? And the opposite, if I feel like trash, then I feel as if everyone in my presence also have less to offer the universe. It is about connecting to higher levels of the soul, the higher (relatively speaking) the person is vibrating at he will be able to feel the interconnectivity between all living things all the more powerfully! We are not just talking about mood.

How unfortunate to disconnect the unit from its whole self, and view it as disintegrated parts! How much abundance there is to go around for all if we were only to realize that everything has its specific place and function, and the existence of another will never put this function in danger! Hoarding money, countries struggling for power, has it yet brought liberty to the world? It won't!

The realization needs to come about through the consciousness of all of our true identities, all manifesting a unique spark in the darkness that is our existence. Of course we needed to fall time and time again in order to learn these lessons. Collectively, it is the right opportunity to learn from the many history lessons that some and most of us have witnessed with our own eyes!

The advancement of technology, and the amount of information circulating through the world in the media, the furthering of education in all areas of the world, it is finally a world community - Facebook, Twitter, Google - the stage is set, no one can claim ignorance of things that have happened to us collectively as a species!

Do not let the messages of the media cheapen the impact of what is being delivered. Take it in its proper context and with the background needed to perceive and understand its meaning. And no, not everything can be known. Adam before the sin was able to see from one side of the world to the other, he knew the chain reaction of every movement, and truly perceived true reality, and he was able to give names to all living things based on their true essence. This means looking at something and perceiving its entirety and all that pertains to that object, including the effect the object is having on everything else, and the effect everything else has back on it. Whoa!

We are not on this level yet, but a person can talk with someone on an iPhone, from one side of the world to the other, and can see each other, talking literally face to face! Isn't that amazing! If someone wants to research a topic he doesn't need to spend years finding a sage in a distant land who knows about the subject; rather, in seconds he can get all of the needed information from Wikipedia without having to exert any effort, reading a summary of a scholar who dedicated his entire life to the subject, and then that summary being summarized into a few paragraphs.

So many keys to our reality are being handed to us, and many souls are lost without the direction necessary to utilize the new wave correctly. Is a theme yet being made clear to you? I hope so. For our sake, I hope so.

FAMILY HISTORY & THE TRUTH OF TRUTH!

My grandfather was born in a small city in Poland called Radzyn. It was a very unique village and amongst other things that were well known about it were the very unique Chassidic masters that lived there. The villagers adored their Rebbes; even the secular had a great respect for them. They weren't the average type of Chassidic masters. Something was truly out of the ordinary in the approach that they followed.

The first of the chain in the dynasty is Rav Mordechai Yosef Leiner from Izbitza. His work, which was collected and written by his grandson, is known as one of the wildest books of the Jewish tradition. Some warn against reading it especially without a guide who has experience in the paths of this approach. The personalities in these Masters' family were extraordinary, writing many works in all areas of the Torah! The Rebbe known as the Radziner Rebbe, Rav Gershon Henoch Leiner was, in addition to being a spiritual guide with miraculous abilities, also a doctor. I myself have seen copies of prescriptions that he sent, written in either English or Latin letters in a beautiful handwriting.

I was only formally introduced to the works of these giants later in high school, when my older brother mailed me a copy of the Mei HaShiloach, 'The Waters of Shiloach'. Even though we did not live a Chassidic lifestyle, this approach to reality was always an undercurrent in our household and was (and still is) already deeply entrenched into our identity.

The stories that I have heard from my father and others in the family about how my grandfather went about his life compare with those of the Chassidic Rebbe's. The jewels were given over, albeit maybe in an unconscious fashion. An open-mindedness they possessed had its sources deep in the roots of the Kabbalistic tradition that the extraordinary Rebbes of this dynasty were uncovering and teaching to the world. They had a remarkable ability to accept and integrate, literally, everything!

There is a book from one of the descendants of the Izbitza Rebbe, from before the Holocaust, who wrote a two-volume work on health called The Great Book of Healing. A more recent work that was written by a descendant who came to England and America, escaping the Holocaust, writes an entire pamphlet of praise and recognition for one of the leaders of the non-Chassidic world of previous generations. For him it was clear, and as well he brings proofs from his own great-uncles' works, that they viewed this sage from the opposing party as a tremendous sage. They had the ability to sift through the politics, and to see the picture for what it is, two sides of a coin! They were very open about it.

This particular family saw no reason to be segregated from the other party, just because they were different. On the contrary, the differences enable each party to clearly see their identity shining strong without needing (from insecurities) to cover all the bases. This is what we excel in, and that is where they do. On a different sort of scale, this book would be like a leader of the arch-capitalists praising the works of Karl Marx!

The approach they convey is more explicitly practical. One such teaching is never to get involved in an argument between leaders, unless you are on the level of refinement of the tzadikim (the truly righteous). Time and time again arguments may occur and before you know it entire communities may be broken up not by what the leaders said, but rather by how the followers riled things up, and mostly, as the holy Rebbe teaches us, simply out of simple emotional insecurities! Before you know it, every infinitesimal piece of dirt is uncovered and the situation blows out of proportion!

Another teaching is regarding disciplining others. How does one go about telling off another for doing wrong? The teaching is based on the saying in the Torah, "Righteousness, righteousness pursue."[21] It interestingly writes the word 'righteousness' twice, so the Rebbe takes from there that first and foremost a person should be meticulous in his pursuit of righteousness, but the person should not be meticulous on someone else and become angry because of their lack of meticulousness. Don't rebuke until you yourself have reached refinement, and once on such a level then you will know what to do in order for the real message of rebuke to settle in to the other in such a way that it will be accepted.

People don't like being told off. While some have become accustomed to criticizing and rebuking others, they first have to ask themselves if it will that actually turn the other into a more responsible individual. It may as well only build more resistance, and cause the other, out of fear of losing identity, to rebel even stronger.

Do we really know all that goes on in another's life? All the struggles and uniqueness they have and are facing daily? From the admonishers perspective it is clear that what is being done is wrong and thank heaven that "Mr. Punisher" is around to make things run smoothly by yelling at the rebuked. If talking from a societal view, yes maybe there needs to be systems of justice set up, however in regards to the delinquent himself and his actual benefit, reprimanding isn't always the answer!

My father told me a story several months ago, that when he was young he went out late with some friends and was out with the car past the curfew my grandparents set. (My father related this story in retort to another youngsters late for curfew story, what the other related was that when they got back from the late bus, the parent, of the friend hanging out with, was there furiously waiting by the bus stop, this person vividly can remember now more than forty years later, how much trouble they got into, and especially the look of anger on the face of the father for not following the set rules!)

My grandfather (of blessed memory) originally from the city of Radzyn (as mentioned above), then in Montreal, stood on the balcony of their second-story apartment waiting for my father to return. As soon as my father pulled into the driveway, without saying anything, my grandfather turned around and finally went to bed. My father related this as something he will never forget!

(My father related this story after hearing another late for curfew story from someone. In that story, when the person and their friend got back home from the late bus, the parent of the friend was furiously waiting by the bus stop. The person, now forty years later, can vividly remember how much trouble they got into, and especially the look of anger on the face of the father for not following the set rules!)
Does the reprimand really teach the true lesson needing to be expressed? My father witnessed an act

of compassion, caring, and concern, that a father has for his son, and it is etched in his memory always. It isn't about the rules, but the expression that needs to be conveyed of the inherent act of love and care he wanted to give his son. Not with demands, but coming from a place of truth and depth.

At the end of the day, parents are worried for the child's welfare, and that is so necessary! But sometimes in the communication of this deep love, the language and vessels of communication used are not administered appropriately, even causing more damage and furthering the child from the parents' love!

Something to think about, how to simply relay a message! I can try to solve and fix all the problems in my family, in the community, and with a most sincere mission of building upstanding good-natured individuals, but the subject of my tyranny doesn't see through the same eyes I do. I can't implant my so-to-speak pure vision of the world, and his due reorganization of his own wrongs into his head!

This is the truth of truths! That sometimes the best-communicated truth doesn't need to be the truth. And the truth will only cause deep harm. Is there any benefit in the child admitting, "Yes, I was past the curfew, yes, I stole the car."? Whatever the given situation, there is a need for seeing past the blocking emotions of hurt self pride, "How can my son, etc."

I am sure others have experienced similar in the course of their lives. The more a parent isn't seeing a greater context than just themselves, and treating their child as an extension of them, without seeing the child for who and what they are as an individual, the parent can completely destroy the child in the name of love and compassion.

Everyone we see has their own map of the world, and if we intend to work with them, to change their map to something more and grandiose, we must stop forcing our outlook onto them, because it will never help them that way. We must find a way to enter their reality and think out their response that they will have as a response to your action. It's a flexibility that takes a bit of overcoming self-involvement, and connecting to the greater good in these situations. How truly profound!

A person must as well learn how to rebuke oneself in such a manner that it will not cause further harm, but be leading to a path of development and growth. This means accepting things as they are,, in the context that they manifest themselves!

The problem of pollution, for example. First and foremost let us accept it as a reality. Respect it for all it has done for us, and just connect to it in a way that a father should for his child. Yelling at things doesn't make the problems go away. I am not delivering a message of indifference but of true desire to see the actual fruits that are expected to come forth from any given situation.

Think in objective mind space, let the right brain take over, in a way that the rubbish people have left on the streets is seen in an artistic fashion, as if placed there amongst the leaves so purposefully and gracefully!

Take this experiment if it is of interest to you: Step 1 - Find ten things that make you mad. Step 2 - Now focus on them in an objective scene as pieces in a system.

Let's give an example: I hate it when the neighbor's dog leaves a mess (to put it very mildly) on the sidewalk, so as I walk by, in my mind I can just look at the mess, and say calmly, "Hmm" and then look around it and say "sidewalk", then look at the grass, just appreciating the items as if placed completely perfectly there.

Another situation I am not so fond of is bugs in close contact. If I see an ant farm making its way into my kitchen, after the initial panic I can take a second and just view the situation. House, plants, sidewalk, fruits, ants, people!

Looking from an eye of objectivity, whether I want to get rid of the ant farm from my house is a different question, but first I accept it as a reality and view it with interest, because from a certain perspective it is quite interesting! Instead of squashing the newly defined enemy, maybe I can view the situation as creatures trapped inside who would do much better being returned to their natural outside surroundings!

Once a friend told me that he had to kill a mouse in his house for the sake of not being cruel to living things. When I asked him how that makes sense, he told me he was referring to his wife! His wife demanded the extermination of the little guy while standing in complete fear on top of a chair in the kitchen, panicking and yelling in fear of being attacked by the cute mouse. I guess sometimes the choice of who the culprit is needs to be made for the sake of peace!

Once again, let the situation be a reality without the labels given by your left brain that assesses what the function of the object of the situation needs precisely to be. Allow the flexibility sometimes to be more than just a reactor of emotions, and really analyze based on what is, and then formulate what to do next.

For example, being caught in the rain, there's nothing you can do about it and yes it would be much more comfortable to just be indoors and dry. But this is a valid face of existence and is currently happening, so allow it and see it in a larger picture – "its cold", "wearing wet clothes", "waiting for the bus", "someone passed by on a motorcycle and splashed me with a stream of cold muddy water!" I can see already how much fun this is going to be for you!

THE SECRET TRUTH

Just because something is true doesn't mean necessarily that it is something that can be expressed as a truth! Things can be proven, factual, known to all as being truth, however their expression into words or other forms of communication, in the format it is now, are not suiting, and in fact take away a bit from that which 'truly' is happening!

The Talmud says that at a wedding although everyone knows what it is that happens after the wedding, whoever talks about it outright, "Even if a heavenly decree for them for seventy good years is sealed, the decree is torn up." (Another opinion says, "They deepen the pits of hell for him!")[22]

This is the concept of modesty. Many, when hearing the word modesty, draw a picture in their mind of some girl wearing a snowsuit in the summer, or an Amish family who are not allowed to have any fun, the jail called modesty. Let me ask you: If it is a truth that after the wedding such-and-such occurs, why (being fair and honest here) is it wrong to talk about it? I am a truth seeker and only speak words of truth, so why not now?

(Have you ever met people who act like this? They only mean good, and good meaning the truth. Like a friend who tells you that you look terrible and then says, "But I'm just telling you the truth!")

What's really so bad about people talking about what is done after the wedding, is that it reduces all that has led up to this grand occasion, and all that will hopefully come in the future of their relationship, into something cheap, a common act, just like all the other animals in the jungle do! Isn't that condensing a bit into just a brief description?

A marriage between a man and a woman is something truly Divine! What can possibly be said about it, and yet it probably is the most popular of subjects that man has ever written on - love stories, poems, music, all trying to convey some deep almost intangible notion. Something hovering just above regular nature, I think it has been termed as 'cloud nine'! So would it be fair for onlookers to describe in layman's speech what is about to happen? Or would that be an understatement!

The fact that they are two individuals embarking on mission together, planning to bring into the world the next generation of responsible individuals with unique character to further fix the world and give pride to those who know them, or the reason why the parents and grandparent stand by in tears of joy, just all can't be simply because of what is not to be talked about that particular night!

So you can ditch your definitions of modesty, and relearn some that will be helpful. Things that are secret, and are then revealed into the open if meant to be secret, can only cheapen those things, taking them out of their context. Modesty is context!

The deepest, most intimate part of the Torah is the book by King Solomon called the Song of Songs. It is a story of love, a back and forth between a lover and the beloved. There is a discussion in the Talmud as to why it can be permissible to be included in the 24 books of the Torah, and it was obviously accepted, since we have it today![23] It is amazing how the most intimate part of the Torah is said in such a way, of a love story! The analogy of the story of course is referring to our relationship with God, so why is it necessary to be expressed in such a fashion?

Once again the 'secret truth' cannot be true if said straight and honest. 'Honesty' really doesn't win in this game, things that are a bit higher than the regular, even higher than cloud nine, cannot merely be relayed with the message blurted flat out.

When I see an advertisement for a book or a lecture series, or anything else that irks me like that, with the intent of discussing faith, love of God, or just about "God", it gives me ample warning to run far away! Talking about it is cheapening it! It really bugs me to hear songs about faith that are just a bit too blunt!

Who doesn't know what is happening on the night of a wedding, but come on, there is so much more than that. As soon as I start to explain to someone else the feelings I have, or things he should be feeling for God, I already missed the point!

The book by one of the Chassidic Rebbes called the Maor Vashamesh, says: What is really secret? Is it the writings of the Kabbalah? Is that what the real secrets are? No, of course not. Rather the things that are really secret are the feelings and elevated thoughts of consciousness one has about the Divine. It is something so deep that it is impossible to relay to another, and the attempt will only be filled with empty meaningless words compared to what is actually being experienced!

I can give you all the writings of the Kabbalists but I can't relay to you things of this secretive nature. It is individual and unique to be experienced by you alone. A great method used by many Jews from all groups is to go out for a period of time to the forests or some other secluded place, and there pour out the heart in longings and personal prayer before the Creator. This is a great and beautiful practice that truly cannot be properly described, so it is wise not to trust the descriptions given from those who attempt to describe it. It's the most secret. That's why it is so deep and beautiful!

I have been getting into poetry lately, and writing music, even art, with these feelings in mind and trying to paint a picture with them through vessels of analogy, and cryptic terms. Through these means, I intend to lead the onlooker into this state of falsehood, where the story just doesn't fit, where the underlying current is just forced, not to reveal itself, but to shout out from behind saying, "follow me, I am here, there is no question!" All areas of creativity, as artists can relate to, are Godly adventures, the inspiration felt is not just from the dopamine, again which would be an understatement!

Art is soul expression; it needs to be accessed from the right brain, which will open you to the beyond of yourself. Not to stay in analytic mode and be expecting to see beyond; it just won't lead to such an experience. Only someone who has previously experienced such feelings can relate. To those who have not yet had the opportunity, just know that it exists, and be ready to receive this state in your life, whenever it may come.

In Judaism there is no concept of God. That which Jews call God is actually just Hebrew for "the Name". We don't even say the name let alone the true essence!

For heaven's sake can it just be that the prohibition of saying the names of God in vain is from a fear that we may be turned into a rabbit?!

Please realize the greater picture. Hear and feel the modesty. It can't be communicated as such, especially not in a place not fitting. Don't say it in the bathroom, because that just is not the place! When stubbing your toes, it's not the right moment!

One of the parts of the Zohar is called The Book of Modesty. They say this is the deepest part of the Kabbalah and almost everything is built upon it. Kabbalah isn't even talking about God, it talks about His names and garments he uses to relate to us with, and even still so much secret surrounds it.

But the point is not to let the secret out, to finally bring to you the secret of Kabbalah, heaven forbid! I want no such part in that! All that I may be expressing isn't of the secret, this is the revealed. The secret is something that will remain secret, that no words will be able to encapsulate or be discussed over a cup of tea. When we talk we say "the Name", that's it! "Oh how was your day?" "Well, thank "the Name", fine!"

This is a purposeful disconnect that was not intended to be distant and uninvolved but rather a preservation of something that I really want, and choose to keep secret! So I use words and descriptions that I can!

There is a story in the Talmud of someone who leads the prayer services, and in the beginning there are certain praises that are mentioned (all according to the Kabbalistic system), and this man went beyond the regular customary verses and added in his own few. As he was about to continue with the rest of the blessing the other rabbis present said to him, "Is that all? You decided to take the initiative of adding some praises, how nice. So you think you can stop there and suffice with that?"[24]

We are talking infinite here! The prayers are set up in a way that every word is in tune with Kabbalistic names correlating to the sefirot, worlds, and actions that God uses to manifest himself to us, none of which can be labeled as God, only a manifestation of Him, for our sake, not His!

Imagine the situation if Einstein, having just finished his theory of relativity with the energy of creativity pulsing through him, walks up to the first person he meets, the janitor in his office, and blabs out his work excitedly and waits for the janitor's reaction. It is hard enough for the janitor to speak German, let alone understand these matters that only the highest and most well trained minds can grasp, and then only with the aid of pages upon pages of equations to the point that they look Einstein in the eye and say, "Wow you have done it!" Anything before that would be an utter de-contextualization of the art being expressed!

It is beyond the truth, which is a preservation of the truth, an interesting concept to grasp but it takes a sensitivity of heart and proper application to use it correctly.

WHERE IS THE SOUL FOUND?

The question is, can the soul be seen with the physical eyes? Is there an actual connection between the spiritual and physical, or is it just feeling-based? Are there any more details or is it just left to the realm of beyond?

The soul, spoken of before, has five parts paralleling the five worlds, and as well, ten sefirot viewed as five parts. Based on the flowing relativity of the Kabbalistic system, it all depends on what is being observed and from what angle! Even if named so, the lowest part of the soul of one person may be on the level of the highest part of another.

The theme of five will be an active participator in this explanation. Any system can be expressed as five according to the Kabbalah. The first of the five is the 'highest' position from which the other four are manifest (as mentioned regarding the worlds, although there are five only four are generally discussed relative to us), which is the state of the One who emanates the four worlds from the state of potential into actuality. This is not the Creator, but the level higher than those that stem from it, which can sometimes be viewed as such (the Creator), although it is not the Infinite Himself, just the clothing, the system being spoken of.

The first of the five also functions as both the bridge between each of the four levels and the bridge between that system of four and the next higher system of four.

Just as the route for us to connect to the Divine is through this channel of perfect individualized separate elements which are the ten sefirot, which are the vessels through which God uses to transmit sustenance to us, so too, the body has the same way to connect to the soul, and in fact every system stemming from inanimate to human, all run by the same system of fives!

So let's start from here and apply the viewing of things in systems of five to the physical world. We have inanimate objects, then vegetative growing things, animals, and man! This is four levels, while the fifth level is that from which all four stem. And as well, in the process, there is always a bridge from one level to the other. From inanimate to vegetative, the bridge is algae. From vegetative to animals, the Kabbalists speak about an animal similar to a dog, that is attached from its belly button to the ground and receives nourishment from the soil, and if cut from the ground, will die. The bridge between animal and man is the monkey. All of this is working in parallel with the four-letter name that is not enunciated but rather intended, concentrated on.

Now, let's apply the system of five to the physicality of a person himself. The lowest is the house that a person lives in, then the clothes they wear, then the actual body, and the fourth is the soul. And to go further, let's take a micro look at a transition between two levels. What would you say is the level in between the physical body and the clothing that is worn by the body?

The hair and nails! Although being part of the body itself, if cut off it doesn't hurt in the slightest. A person can even sell their hair to another to use as a wig! Funny type of clothing, but it is natural clothing that can be taken from the hair of an animal such as a sheep, and functions as if it were a garment. Only the roots will hurt if pulled at.

How about the transition between the clothing and house? This is a tent, made out of cloth! It is a house on the one hand yet not made from stones and cement, so it can even be worn!

In this system as demonstrated every single aspect is further able to be broken into four and then the fifth which is really the lowest from the higher system, but in relation to the four it is a different reality which includes and encompasses the other lowers.

One approach of looking at the body is, (from outward to inner), skin, muscle tissue, sinews, bone, and then blood is the fifth. Let me preempt this explanation with the Torah's prohibition against eating blood of an animal, the reason given, "Because the blood is the soul"! [25] I know from my personal experience of being a shochet, a ritual slaughterer of birds, that it is a commandment to cover the blood of every wild animal or bird slaughtered properly with dust, in order for the proper spiritual correction to be done; this is done with a blessing on the commandment to cover the blood with dust.

The blood that requires covering is called the "quarter blood of the soul." Only the first quarter of spilled blood is what contains the lowest aspect of the soul, and is treated with respect and along with the rest of the blood, it is forbidden to be eaten.

While it is the highest of the physical elements, being the most refined aspect of the blood manifested in physicality, it is the lowest in the chain of the soul system it is coming from, where it is called the "nefesh of the nefesh" (refer to Sefira Chart in the chapter 'The Levels of Soul'). It is the lowest of the 10-sefira subset within the lowest sefira, from a system within a system.

And in this manner of one system to another system, spirituality is manifest in the physical world! From the rocks all the way to the highest spiritual world the same pattern is followed, with the guidelines so given. And every step can be dissected and broken into systems in of itself of tens, fives, threes, until infinity!

A common example used to describe these levels in the human lifespan is called pregnancy, nursing, and greatness (or adulthood). The same pattern described earlier of the system of three, beginning, middle, and end. However in other scenarios where an adult is growing but is in the infant stages of his adult growth, he may be referred to as being in the stage of nursing of adulthood, the beginning of the end!

Just as one finishes middle school and is the grandest most mature specimen on the campus, he is then thrown into a new status in high school called freshman, corresponding to the pregnancy stage. And once again from high school to university, and from there to achieving seniority in a job, the same system applies. In relationships as well there are infant stages of the relationship, then closer levels, and even closer levels, all being able to be categorized (although it is not necessary to categorize) into the universal system.

Have you ever noticed yourself transferring from one state to another, with the previous state being in complete view, but with the new scenario putting you into a dizzying position? This is a state of growing (relatively) from the light of one level to the darkness and initial hardships of the next!

The physical is an actual meeting place of this level of soul through the medium of the blood, where we are given the opportunity to be a vehicle (for the light which is coming from higher), including in ourselves this light in order to properly utilize the physical dimensions.

Even in the spiritual realms, those of the angels, there are different levels of angels that correlate to the different worlds. They, however, are not as fortunate as us in our ability to live and express our free will in the physical regard. They are in fact jealous of us, especially regarding the secrets of the Torah. They were thrown into shock that this wisdom was being handed over to such a lowly earthly participant. What they did not understand is that we, and our physical bodies, are the level of bridging between the material and non-material worlds.

That's why all the Jewish events, as the jokes go and the truth of the matter is, are all based on food! Every joyous occasion from a wedding to a circumcision, are all initiated over a blessing on a glass of wine, followed after by a joyous feast of food. Every opportunity we have is meant to be a channel to the uplifting of the physical.
Ours is not a tradition of shunning the pleasures but of being able to consciously incorporate them into our higher being through using their energies to do our heavenly mission here! The angels just have their

mission to do, but we have more!

This is obviously a responsibility that requires balance. If wine needs me to uplift the sparks of holiness within it, then I should drink lots of it, right? The fight is there between the soul and the body. Undirected, the body can get itself into lots of trouble, acting more like an animal than even the animals would ever be caught doing. This knowledge from behind the scenes of why our food is here, doesn't give us free reign to scoffindulge and destroy the body or the natural environment. It is meant to bring a further layer of consciousness and mindfulness in our every action from the Godlike to the mundane, which in turn makes eating a spiritual experience, lifting it to its original source! Real delicious!

In the next section, we are going to continue with this theme of food, with a practical look at being conscious about food itself in the context of a hopefully integrated life.

A WHOLE HEALTHY LIFE

There are many factors that need to be taken into account to make the right choices in actualizing potential. I am fortunate to be a part of a group of like-minded individuals led by a Chassidic Rebbe, who makes it his business to teach the public the necessary wisdom and tools needed to really achieve that which each person has come to this world for. This wisdom and tools are called the Four Foundations of Pilzno, which everyone human being, regardless of religion, ideology, nationality, or culture needs to have set up in life in order to succeed. The Rebbe has worked with many people from diverse backgrounds and has set them up on their merry way of self-actualization.

THE FOUR FOUNDATIONS

While there is a handbook of the foundations in circulation I would just like to summarize certain things, so that the reader will know where to search if necessary. The four are:

(1) Guidance - To have a guide, mentor, or access to people who have successfully done what you are currently trying to achieve and can help you formulate a vision and reach your goals. As the previous Rebbe said, "Speaking to those who have already accomplished that which you are trying to do can save you lifetimes!" This corresponds to the world of Atzilut (refer to chart in the chapter 'The Levels of Soul').

(2) Knowledge - To study the appropriate information needed to reach your goals and to grow toward your infinite potential throughout life. This includes spiritual texts or relevant secular wisdoms. Even if there is no particular need for the knowledge, sometimes it is important for the sole sake of being able to relate to a wider group of people, while without this knowledge your ability to communicate would be limited.

Creativity is part of this, which is making sure to come up with novelties in the realm of ideas, or a song, for example. The previous Rebbe was careful to write a novel thought every night before going to sleep, just to keep the creative juices flowing! This corresponds to the world of Beriyah.

(3) Relationships – To surround yourself with a group of like-minded individuals who you can rely on for support in pursuit of your dreams, building healthy friendships, business contacts, and maintaining these connections. Family relationships are obviously included here. This corresponds to the world of Yetzirah.

(4) Financial and Physical Health - Having all the support, love, knowledge, and guidance, won't be of service to someone who is breaking under a financial burden, or suffering from easily avoidable diseases. This corresponds to the world of Asiyah.

All the above elements need to be in place for one to begin drawing down that which is higher than the four, the fifth, the source of the four, which is beyond the scope of this material world. These outlined fundamentals apply to every human in any situation. They are a must for growth, and if one is seeking spiritual wisdom and has issues in these areas, such as health or finances, then the teachings won't truly enter his being to really elevate him in a spiritual way, it will only appear as such.

The Baal Shem Tov, the founder of the Chassidic movement, said that a small hole in the body corresponds to a big hole in the soul! Of essential importance is our responsibility to our body and its protection. Not for the sake of the body in of itself, but for the unification that occurs – the relationship of the soul (the male) with its counterpart, the body (the female)! One without the other is out of place.

How beautiful can the body be if used in the service of something higher, how much sweetness and joy can be felt through this experience. If treated properly it gives so much to the whole of the body-soul unit, letting in high feelings and deep emotions, intuition and sensitivities, a gentleness, if given the chance. Allowing the whole to be a chariot moving forward in the sunset like two lovers, blissfully, enjoying each other's company, listening to their aspirations and harshest moments of trial. Yearning together for higher than is possible, willing the heavens to split open and draw them forwards, to beyond.

This is where the soul and body can be in our lives - communicating to one another and sharing messages from beyond. Give the body its chance to be the physical channel that all the worlds are accessing the material through! Build your body in this Divine way; strengthen the muscles literally, in order to be more of a fitting means of communication for the universe!

REAL ORGANIC!

I have, for a long while, been attracted to wholeness in systems; it has been a part of my development. Way before knowing anything about an "integrated lifestyle", such as mind-body relationships, or of nutrition, I remember firmly believing that whole milk products, since they were whole, must be very healthy for the body (whereas everyone else was saying whole milk products were fattening), so at that time I would enjoy a day's ration of a loaf of white bread and a whole stick of butter. (Little did I know what negative effects that meal had for me!) This was still, however, a step up from my childhood diet of chicken fingers or fish sticks (for example), things that were fully taken out of their element, processed, and then introduced in a kid-friendly fashion.

As I continued on the path, I began eating all different parts of the chicken, such as the wings, and not just the breast, trying to chew the parts that were a bit more stringy, as well specifically eating the fatty parts of a piece of beef. I was opening myself to being more accepting to a holistic view in this area of food; I changed my observation from "yuck", to having an interested curiosity, and wanting to see how the whole food (so to speak) would taste. It wasn't always the most nutritionally sound approach, but it was part of my exploration.

Since at the time, I completely accepted meat and dairy to be a standard staple of the human diet, I began to develop a curiosity about the process involved in the production of the products. I became set on learning and practicing as a shochet, a Jewish Kosher slaughterer. I didn't want my relationship to be left at the stage where I purchase a Styrofoam package with plastic wrap around what we are told is a chicken. How did it get there? Where is it from? Who slaughtered it? Was it healthy?

I had a true passion for holism and decided to pursue this as a means of making a living, hoping to do it on a farm of organic animals. Although at the time I didn't know anything whatsoever of real organic, the general theme spoke to me, that being of well-cared for sensitively handled animals. This was my dream at the time, but I barely told anyone of such ideas; I just stored them away until the right time would present itself. And before I knew it, I found myself a place close to my school, and began learning all the laws and details of shechita, Kosher slaughter.

People who knew me were in shock. "You a shochet? Why not something more calm and less bloody? You just don't look the type." And I really didn't look the type - a boy from Canada who only saw chickens in the movies, basically.

I remember when they brought our group of students for the first slaughtering. It was something that I needed time to get a handle on, quite traumatic for me actually. We were behind an old apartment building next to the dumpsters, and they brought three chickens for every one of us. I kindly opted to go last while the other first-timers got up to the slaughtering like pros. Whether they did them successfully or not was something else. I remember that mine were all done correctly the first time.

It didn't end there. Then we needed to, as mentioned previously, let the blood drain onto dust and cover it with a blessing again with dust. Afterwards, we opened the insides to see if they were of kosher standards, not the fondest of memories. Finally, after sorting through the insides it was ready to be taken home, but not to be cooked and eaten, but to salt the remainder of blood from within the flesh of the animal.

My study partner at the time, not one of the slaughterers, helped me to start the salting and cleaning at his home, and then I went to crash at my place with a chill and a pounding headache. What an interesting experience! This all was part of my dream; I just now needed to get myself used to the described scenario!

Surprisingly, I didn't stop my intake of chicken or meat from this occurrence, and with my new skill and knowledge had more of an appreciation of what every household would take for granted. This meant a lot to me and helped me to build a mindfulness in what I was eating.

I as well wanted to get more in touch with other areas of our food sources, so I volunteered for a short time in a newly started organic farm. There I was introduced to things that I knew were beyond the scope of what my fellow Torontonians would in any way call normal. Although some things were new and strange, I was truly interested in learning as much as I could, and I tried (as difficult as it may have been for me at the time) to be open minded.

One new thing I learned about was their system for human waste composting. Even today when I mention this to anyone unfamiliar with the topic, they just cannot even fathom it, and frankly toss the idea, not seeing it as a great alternative to what we are doing now! Does anyone really know what happens to our waste after it is flushed down? Does anyone know if that ends up having an effect on our health, or if it comes anywhere near our drinking water?

For some strange reason society is led to believe that the government knows entirely what they are doing especially in regards to the health of its citizens! It is widely taken for granted that there are special men in uniforms cleaning and purifying every single molecule of our foods, and resources, with a federal stamp of approval on it.

Have you ever wondered where it all ends up? Find out what is going on in your area how is the system set up, and where the waste goes!

The way the human waste composting (based on the Permaculture approach) was explained to me is that nothing goes to waste, every aspect of the system works together with the others, so it is not necessary to send the trash several kilometers out of smell's way, leaving the mess for others to worry about. What an amazing approach! Even the most disintegrated part of the human body's cycle is completely utilized positively! It even is known to be the best type of compost (if done properly).

This immediately spoke to me as something very in line with the Kabbalistic teachings discussed, and is an analogy of correction: When a person eats food it gives him energy and nourishes him with the vitamins and minerals in the food. The body then extracts whatever it can and then expels the un-digested matter along with other things, even things harmful for the body, so as not to be lugging around unnecessary matter.

This waste, in regards to the human as a system, is that which doesn't have any purpose in the state of being outside of the human system, and is merely waste which needs to be hidden and distanced. Obviously no further rectification can come about in this state of being!

The Permaculture system is a huge lesson for us in our life, regarding those things, no matter how far out, even the deepest darkest evil, and their real true potential for correction. They can actually be used as fertilizer for future growth. This is a lesson that needs to be brought out of the books and more into the way we interact, specifically how to interact with our physical environment, as we can learn from the Permaculture system.

POLLUTION & REVOLUTION

Pollution is most definitely a concern. How much longer will we all be able to contently ship around our trash to some distant landfill just forgetting all about it? Nothing is forgotten! Everything will come around for its correction, for its true integration into a larger system, whenever that may be. Pushing off the matter is just closed minded, and narrow.

Everyone in the right time, starting from whatever level of environmental integration, can begin somewhere to implement active conscious global living. Taking the responsibility where one can in their lives, to better the planet we live in.

I went to the store recently and purchased a kilogram of whole grains. When I returned home to prepare my meal I noticed that the grains were infested with insects. Ok. I accepted it with love from the heavens, and went out to the field near my house and emptied its contents with the insects into the empty field. Later on, when returning to the store I purchased it from, I mentioned that the remaining sacks of grain were also infested just as mine was. They said, "Well, if you bring it back, we will refund your money."

Now, whether or not the right thing to do is to return the contents and receive the refund, I was very disturbed by the accepted approach of both the buyers and sellers. Can I really hold the store accountable for me not checking the grains? If it was a product of very heavily industrialized nature, then yes. Maybe with those substances that are labeled as "foods" there can be some question of refund, if the item goes bad in the twelfth year before the fifteen year due date is up.

As well, I was purchasing a dozen eggs, and I saw that several were broken. I asked the cashier if she can just divide the number by how many good ones I am taking. Her response was that I must take another case and that the broken cases get sent back to the farm, where they will be discarded, and taken off the tab of the retail store!

The world has forgotten how to communicate. Big business pushes all the details under the rug as companies go more and more global with higher stocks, bigger investors, all the while completely missing the basic elements of sensitivity due their own product.

How much longer can this go on?

While discussing all these matters with my Rebbe, he told me, "We aren't going back, there is only forwards." The back-to-the-land movements may have their place, but the world (post industrial revolution) will never be the same, for the positive and the negative. What businesses do need to learn is how through technology they can both profit and build the world responsibly into the utopia it is one day destined to be!

To just mention briefly, the first murder in human history was Kain murdering his brother Hevel (Abel). According to the Kabbalah, Kain who was a worker of the land, represented the female side, the "what is" (the spherical) of things. His brother, who was a shepherd, stood for the side of integration, the middle aspect that unites the right to the left.

Originally, I looked at the story as a story of the fight between the mass agricultural movements killing off everything in its wake, especially the jobs (literally and metaphorically) of the shepherd who uses the land in harmony with his flock.

This was how I viewed the story, but the Kabbalah is saying that the murder wasn't on the masculine side, but rather was on the aspect of integration that can allow the merging worlds to live harmoniously. That nature and technology can be used together in ways that will not be of damage to either's resulting potential.

Our own story is as well part of this original murder. We are still doing the soul correction on many levels through our efforts today. To build a bridge between the worlds, this is where the future must take us.!

It is time for the hippies (or at least one of them), who are preaching many beautiful concepts, to put on a suit and tie, and be able to communicate with the world unfamiliar with an organic lifestyle, to give them feasible ideas to limit waste or how to go about supporting local produce (without them getting their hands dirty. Just yet!).

We must understand how integral each of our unique roles are to all of us. I couldn't be who I am if the opposite wasn't who they are, respectfully giving the appropriate space necessary. It must be understood how no actual fight exists between the green and the big business! The integration was murdered, and now it is our job to fix it!

WHOLESOME PROCESSED FOODS

There is a beautiful teaching of the sages of the Talmud:

*Rabbi Achai the son of Yeshaya said: One who takes
wheat from the market, to what is he likened? To a child
whose mother has died and he is brought to the houses of
nursemaids but is not satisfied!*

*One who takes bread from the market, to what is he likened?
That he has dug a grave and been buried!*

*One who eats from his own, is comparable to a child who is
raised on his mother's breast, that through the birth itself
the mother's blood begins to turn into milk and in fact, it
is the child's birth itself that causes its being satisfied from
his mother's milk, whereas being nursed from others, the
baby is not satisfied from it since he was not the cause of this
nourishment.*[26]

The Sages are giving us a profound understanding
of the necessary ideal relationship needing to occur
with the most mundane of things such as the bread
we eat. It is most definitely not enough to be living a
spiritual life and not putting any concern as to how
close to the sources one may be. The message is clearly
a call to process, and to build a relationship with those
things in my reality. They are speaking in harsh terms
against such a life lacking in closeness and integration.
Who was it that baked my bread? I am not referring

to whether the bread is of whole grain or not, this is a whole different concept. How close to the process am I?

People are living completely disassociated from their lives and their problems. A person sees a therapist and wants the therapist to fix them. There is a pain in the body, or emotions of a person, so they get a prescription from the more than ready pharmaceutical companies (who happen to be one of the most profitable businesses these days) all without ever once even confronting the issue that is going on within them which started from the very actions and habits the person has been doing to themselves!

The Talmud is right! Is it not as if one has dug a grave and been buried? This intensely strong disassociation of the self is writing the self off to death. Death for sure, of the intimate relationship between the fine soul, and its interaction with this struggling body, that even the mind is trying to send messages to just alert that it may need some water, but instead there is a special pill for that! Awareness and an appreciation of all things no matter how outside of the self, seeing things in their rightful context and place, not just using and abusing!

How important the process is to us! I personally enjoy taking the time and preparing homemade raw sauerkraut with organic cabbage and real sea salt. This age-old food is full of healthy probiotics that we all so badly need (in our trigger finger antibiotic giving culture), it helps fill our gut with micro-flora that help us to more easily break the food we eat down and process the good and bad parts found in our diet, aiding our digestion tremendously.

I do it, not only as a means of preparing food to eat, but as well intend the process to be that of a connection and relationship building that I want to develop. I look at it as a meditation, and all through the time that it takes for the sauerkraut to liven up, it is feeding on the micro flora and reacting with things that are in the home environment, so whereas I am not yet able to be growing my own yet, I can still be fortunate enough to be part of the process!

SIMPLY SPEAKING!

The general rule, I believe, in regards to food is to just keep things simple. As author Michael Pollan says, "Eat food mostly plants not too much", and that just about sums things up doesn't it! His books are a great resource for the real scoop on today's foods, and how to get back in touch with our basics.

The problem, as I know from my own experience, is the ability to relearn what a simple clean diet truly is! In order to just be simple these days one might need some complexities in hand. All the foods are marketed to an unknowing audience. If it has something terrible in it, they will advertise that it doesn't have another poison in it, so that people will assume the food company has their best intentions in mind by putting the ingredients on the label. And if there are words that you can't pronounce than suspect it may be that way in order for you to not understand, and once again put your trust in the food companies.

Never listen to the claims for health on any products they are just meant to mislead people. Stay away from hydrogenated or partially hydrogenated fats, and that also means margarine. I joke with my sister-in-law, that when her daughter hit her head and started bleeding another woman quickly put some margarine on the wound and it stopped the bleeding! Exactly!

FRUITS & VEGETABLES

There are, thank heavens, quite an amazing amount of variety to choose from any time of year. Get in tune with the seasonal produce and let your body easily work with those climate's seasonal appropriate fruits. All the different vegetables and fruits have different energetic and nutritional values to them. I don't like the playing favorites game of "this is the most healthy." The body needs an assortment, and what is found in one item isn't found in the other, so choose from a variety, find what you like and mix it up, there is no reason for things to get boring. Learn to rely on fruits and vegetables as a main part of the diet, not potato chips, and cheese curls!

GRAINS

It is very confusing for the average family to comprehend what the whole grain scene is talking about; they think it may just be the whole wheat bread. Not exactly! So many cultures ate a diet that was accompanied by a whole grain, buckwheat, whole oats, wheat berries, brown rice, quinoa, barley, and several others.

Today we are inundated by white processed flour, which is missing the other parts that would constitute its wholeness. In its denatured form it doesn't have the complete and necessary components to truly fuel the body in the appropriate ways. The whole grains also keep the person fuller longer and are easier on the person's blood sugar level. They, in their entirety, contain essential vitamins and minerals that the body needs in order to function its best. Get used to cooking with grains and vegetables, try different combinations depending on the season, and spice it accordingly.

In no way whatsoever does a more whole-foods approach to eating mean bad tasting. Find some good recipe books, and integrate this whole grains approach into your repertoire.

NUTS, SEEDS, BEANS, & GRAINS

One amazing thing that nuts, seeds, beans, and grains have in common is they all have an enzyme inhibitor coating them. This inhibitor prevents the seed from growing before it is the right time. In order to help ease the digestion it is recommended to soak them for several hours to overnight. This way the body can focus on what it is meant to be doing without having to fight foreign elements that slow the breakup and absorption of the essential nutrients.

Nuts and seeds are a great source of protein and healthy fats, and as a reminder: Fats don't make you fat! Fats are incredibly important for our brain and cell function, so make sure you are getting enough good wholesome fats.

Lentils and beans are also a great part of a meal, and are good for the protein they contain as well.

DAIRY, EGGS, & FISH

It is very common in the western cultural diet to place
the main focus of meals on these animal products.
In regards to health, a person must take into serious
account as to whether or not these foods work well
with their system. I spent a month on an organic
goat farm doing some shepherding, and took to my
advantage the raw milk, and goat cheeses, really
nothing like it in the world!

However, even though it was very healthy and at the
highest levels of organic nature, it was causing me
trouble for my stomach and was having an effect on my
allergies that until then were more or less in a regular
state. I needed to learn for myself that dairy at that time
in my life wasn't working for me. I am not ruling it
out indefinitely but for now that's where I stand in my
dynamic self-process.

Growing up I had aan accepted education regarding
the health benefits of dairy and its necessity in helping
to build strong bones, and prevent osteoporosis. While
I am not a doctor or a scientist, I was very grateful to
see the work of Dr. Colin Campbell, that discusses
the relationship between cancer increase and dairy
intake. Energetically this is a very sound theory, that
just as a calf needs the mother's milk to grow and
reach its natural strength and height, taking these very
nurturing and growing substances in a situation where

not looking to be growing and nurturing the further growth in the body, will inevitably lead to the growths of things which may not be so helpful for the person, such as cancer. His book is called The China Study.

A great alternative I have personally found to milk is almond milk. I was amazed at how simple it was to make it myself, and when I feel the need for some oats with milk I use some homemade almond milk. And regarding the cows that are milked, if the cows are milked when pregnant there is a surplus of hormones that are found in the milk and this as well can be an instigator for dangerous growths in the body. The film Forks Over Knives is a great resource for more information in this matter.

Whereas it is very accepted to eat these things with every meal, just take the time to see how it reacts with your own body, and what can be used as an alternative that will be easier on the body as well as on the environment.

MEAT & POULTRY!

I have personal experience from the poultry industry, having spent several months apprenticing at a giant plant that slaughtered eighty thousand chickens a day, five days a week. Believe me the days were long! It was an eye opener, and while at the plant I began limiting my meat and poultry intake.

This was not based on the standards of the kosher levels, but rather from the amount of process and big business involved, the hard working hours the men in the factory put in, and not at the highest pay, or with the greatest benefits. Some said that they wouldn't have any other way to make a living now, having been there for some years. I didn't want to be a part of the stress of the industry almost primarily for the sake of the workers there. And the chickens, well with eighty thousand daily you can't expect them to be treated with too much dignity! I don't even want to know where they all came from but without fail another daily shipment of trucks and trucks of birds were waiting for us as we were about to start our day.

From the spherical view discussed previously, it is "what it is"! And on top of the current big business factory farming there is still a necessity for doing things in line with the Jewish law that the slaughter must take place in the most precise place in a manner that the animal shouldn't suffer. I only plea that the consciousness expand beyond the slaughter itself, to include the way it was grown, more of an "upright" influence into the situation at hand which is in the chaos of the spherical realms.

In what it is, for a family to serve their children such a meal with such a chicken is not wrong, rather the scenario can be improved and uplifted to encompass more than just what is!

I know that I don't want to be actively involved in further cruelty that is dished out from the big business animal product industries, not being part of the global deforestation for the purpose of making room for our animals to graze, so we can sell meat at a cheaper price and be able to eat it more often!

And regarding health claims, take a multivitamin, and a b12 vitamin. If you are of a nature that really you just need meat to function well, either find organic close to the source meat and poultry, or for those who just can't exist without it and crave it strongly, such as blood type O, you can take an Ayurvedic Indian herb called Coleus Forskohlii that tells the body it is satiated from meat!

The Talmud speaks about such a thing as energetic influence, I recall it mentions the use of small fish (since they have a multiplying and reproducing factor) to be eaten when ill in order to quickly bounce the body back to health in the same manner that the small fish reproduce and multiply![27] But back then there was no such thing as growth hormones, or pesticides, so just keep this in mind when purchasing animal products. We don't want to actively bring particles that underwent tremendous trauma, fear, disease, or other ingredients that are not labeled as foods, into our genetic makeup.

In order to happily and healthily function we need to ingest materials that have been under those same influences we so desire for ourselves. Just because these things are not seen to the eye, doesn't mean that they aren't having an effect on our systems.

AFTERWORD ON FOODS

Remember the universal rule discussed earlier that 'wherever you are found that's where you can start'. Start uniquely from that place; do not jump all the steps immediately to live a completely whole life, for that would be very inorganic and not lasting. Introduce slowly over time changes into your reality that will bring you more and more in touch with the unity of our reality that we all experience together. Of great necessity in this transition is the ongoing work together with a health and lifestyle coach to achieve success in your desired goals.

CONTEXT FRIENDLY

We can't always be eating or doing those world fixing activities all the time. Be sensitive to the scenario at hand and as to whether, for example, your using plastic cups will be of the correction or of a destructive action to the given scenario, taking into account the greater picture!

As I left the organic farm where I learned about Permaculture, and was heading to live in an apartment building, the leader of the group told me, "Don't worry, not every time in a person's life is right for doing all these recycling endeavors."

The time will come, just be sensitive and receptive for the right time, realizing that the present is great for all that it is, and will be all the better in the future with further correction. This is the chaos and the rectification!

TO SUM UP

The purpose of this work has been to impact, inspire, and influence you and your perception as to what an integrated existence means and how it can be achieved in your own life, as seen through the Kabbalistic system which details and gives insight into all the trends we can see in our world view, and even higher above, and from where to begin initiating change, in order to turn this world into a Godly dwelling place, through connection to the grand universal purpose and allowing it to permeate every aspect of our lives, even down to the food we eat.

We have discussed systems and patterns that are repetitively shown in our reality, and are detailed in the Kabbalistic system. The use of these Kabbalistic patterns is key in order to move ahead in a progressive positive way for all sides involved in the process of growth, meaning literally every single particle that makes up the universe that is known to us, and even beyond that in the spiritual realms, until Infinity!

ACKNOWLEDGMENTS

Bringing these ideas into reality, onto the page, and into your hands was the work of a number of people. First I would like to thank all of my teachers who are constantly inspiring me to new higher levels of consciousness.

Thanks to my family, friends, and community for giving me their presence and acceptance all of the time.

Specifically on this project, special thanks go out to my editor, Baruch Z'ev Olenick, and my graphics and layout pro, Yoel Bender of dubmethod.com.

And to my Mom and Dad, thanks.

Please feel free to contact me at mordechaifleising@gmail.com with any questions or comments, and to find out about online classes and continuing education.

www.mordechaifleising.com

FOOTNOTES

[1] Talmud Bavli, Gittin 6b

[2] Talmud Bavli, Bava Basra 58b, Vayikrah Rabbah 20:2

[3] Midrash Beraishis Rabbah, 8:10

[4] Talmud Bavli, Chagiga 12a, Sanhedrin 100a

[5] Beraishis, Lech Lecha, 15:8

[6] Iyov 19:26

[7] Sefer Yetzirah, 1:4

[8] Eitz Chaim, Attiah edition pg 9

[9] Talmud Bavli, Sanhedrin 37a

[10] Tehilim 115:17

[11] Talmud Bavli, Makos 11a

[12] Zohar, Chaya Sarah, 46 in the Sulam edition.

[13] Sichos Haran 267

[14] Beraishis 2:15

[15] Midrash Koheles Rabbah 1:13

[16] Talmud Bavli, Baba Kama 50a

[17] Prophets Shmuel 2, 14:14

[18] Ilan Ramchal Chapter 10:4

[19] Talmud Bavli, Sanhedrin 90a

[20] Jerusalem Talmud, Yoma 1a

[21] Devarim, Shoftim 16:20

[22] Talmud Bavli, Kesubos 8b

[23] Mishnah Teharos, Yadayim 3:5, Vilna print 73a.

[24] Talmud Bavli, Berachos 33b

[25] Devarim 12:23

[26] Avos D'Rebbi Nosson 31:1, see Binyan Yehoshua there.

[27] Talmud Bavli, Berachos 40a

NOTES

NOTES

NOTES

NOTES

NOTES

NOTES

CPSIA information can be obtained at www.ICGtesting.com
Printed in the USA
LVOW132043190213

320808LV00003B/777/P